A connect.faith

Anthology

Editors

Debra Bronkema
Steve Berg

A connect.faith Anthology
ISBN: Softcover 978-1-960326-35-5
Copyright © 2023 by Debra Bronkema, editor

Parson's Porch Books is an imprint of Parson's Porch & Company (PP&C) in Cleveland, Tennessee. PP&C is a self-funded charity which earns money by publishing books of noted authors, representing all genres. Its face and voice is **David Russell Tullock** (dtullock@parsonsporch.com).

Parson's Porch & Company *turns books into bread & milk* by sharing its profits with the poor.

www.parsonsporch.com

Anthology

Contents

Acknowledgements:

First and foremost, Thank you to everyone who submitted their work to the Anthology project.

Thank you to the Creativity lab participants of connect.faith, for giving us the idea, to Hudson River Presbytery for supporting our concept from the beginning, to Brian Allain and Writing for your Life for helping us get the word out about the opportunities of connect.faith, to JoAnna Tivnan for putting the Administrative side of the project together, to Dylan Bronkema for fresh eyes to proof the project as it neared the finish line.

We are grateful for the experience of working together!

The connect.faith team

Why an Anthology?

This anthology comes to you from connect.faith, an organization made up of people who are looking for a place to exercise their spirituality through creativity and justice. We see a world that has put walls around Christianity that seems to try to keep people out. Here, in this Anthology, we are giving people a chance to share their literature, their stories, their poems, their memories in their version of what it means to write progressive Christian literature. We hope you will find your own story in their words, and know that we are on a journey together to spread God's love in this broken and hurting world.

In Christ's Love,

Pastor Debbie Bronkema

A Prayer to Begin

by Lauren Burdette

God, grant me the courage to begin.

Your holy fire to burn within me
Your cooling waters to calm and center me
Your roots to ground me
Your wind to awaken me.

May I allow my fullness to expand,
Into the light and onto the page.
May we dance,
Into the light,
Onto the page.

May these be mine:
Courage. Humility.
Confidence. Trust.
Joy. Hope. Curiosity.
Freedom. Openness.
Strength.
Wonder.
Love.
Love.
Love.

Lauren Burdette draws breath in Pittsburgh, PA. She connects with others through writing and her work as a spiritual director.

A New Day

by Debra J.K. Bronkema

She didn't have an easy childhood.

Parents fighting, finally divorcing, which had been a relief.

Holidays split – everyone keeping count of their time down to the minute. No one actually watching her find ways to make people laugh so she wouldn't cry.

Growing up, no one in her family talked about God. But she heard other people. She thought she knew what they meant. She knew there was supposed to be somebody, but it seemed pretty clear to her that she wasn't part of any plan.

At 18, she found someone to save her, and moved out.
Except he didn't. She came home to find him entertaining someone else in her place.

After that happened, she decided to give life one more chance. She decided to give God a chance to show up, though she did everything she could to make it not happen.

She dressed in ripped jeans and put a hooded sweatshirt over her head. She walked into the fanciest church at the center of the town, saying to herself, 'This is it – this is my last try. If you are real God, someone will see me, and somehow – I'll know that it is you.'

If I had known her then, and she'd told me her plan - I would have been nervous.

At the door, a man greeted her with the words "Welcome Home"

A woman came up to her, saying, "Oh dear, you look cold."

And she realized she was. She was soaking wet from the rainstorm she hadn't paid attention to. The woman grabbed a blanket, and gave it to her, saying, "Here, come in and sit with me and my family. It's much warmer inside."

She sat, listened to the people sing and say words. Through it all, she had a sense that something was happening, that these people, they saw her, and they wouldn't stop seeing her. And she relaxed into what turned out to be a brand
new day.

Rev. Dr. Debbie Bronkema serves as Pastor of Pleasantville Presbyterian Church, and leader of the New Worshiping Community, connect.faith, an online community where creativity, spirituality and justice meet. She has published three books, Finding Manna, Midweek Meditations, and the latest entitled Writing toward wholeness: exploring creativity and spirituality. She leads retreats and workshops on Creativity and Spirituality online and all over the country. Visit her at debbiebronkema.com.

"Shed Light"

by Steve Berg

A cloak of darkness hangs over the earth
That claims we're defined by the place of our birth
We don't like from where you came
And we will never be the same

Remove the cloak and now you see
That they, from there, are just like we
The more we seek to understand their ways
The sooner we will get to better days

Shed the cloak and end the hate
So we can learn to tolerate
Shed the light o'er all the earth
So we can see each other's worth

Steve Berg is an engineer by education, a construction manager by trade, and a poet by no stretch of the imagination. He and his wife recently moved from New York to Maine.

"Bury the Hatchet"

by Jenny Gehman

My husband and I have been trying to leave home for four years now. Trying to leave the very place we felt called to for life.

Funny how that happens. Or sad.

A job loss in November 2016 ushered in what we call our weeping years. After 20 years of service, my husband was let go. It was a financial decision, difficult for those who needed to make it and a devastating blow to us at the time. The pain was compounded by the fact that we live on the property of this ministry. Sensing a lifetime call, we built our home here 26 years ago with every intention to stay.

It's hard to heal in the land of your hurt. At least it has been for us. Every day we look out our windows or walk out our back door to face the life we no longer have. We see other people seemingly living the life for which we long. The reminders of our losses are all around us, so we've done what most pained people do. We've sought a way out. In multiple ways and on multiple days, we've tried to leave. Tried, but failed.

It's felt similar to the Apostle Paul's experience recorded in Acts 16:6-8. He and his companions had a plan to go into Asia, but the Holy Spirit forbade them. They tried another way, "but the Spirit of Jesus did not allow them" to go there either.

Has Jesus ever opposed you like this? It's very annoying! With the Spirit blocking our escape routes, we remain here — longing for community but resisting the one outside our door. We'd prefer a new one, please. One that is nice and shiny where we can avoid (at least for a brief spell) the real work of love, forgiveness and grace. But that doesn't seem to be the way of God for us. Is it for anyone? I seriously doubt it.

All of this leads me to a phrase I woke up to the other week: Bury the hatchet. When words greet me in the predawn hours I know to pay attention to them. I crawled out of bed and did a quick online search.

Grammarist says: "The phrase 'bury the hatchet 'comes from a ceremony performed by Native American tribes when previously warring tribes declared peace. When two tribes decided to settle their differences and live in harmony, the chief of each tribe buried a war hatchet in the ground to signify their agreement."

I read that after a 1794 treaty between the United States and Great Britain, John Jay wrote to Lord Grenville: "May the hatchet be henceforth buried forever, and with it all the animosities."

I picture a gravestone over the site of buried hatchets reading: Herein lie resentments, wrongs and misunderstandings.

A hatchet can symbolize cutting all ties and connection with something or someone. It's also a weapon used to cause harm.

My husband and I felt the fall of the ax in 2016, cutting us off from our purpose, place, provision and people. I'm sorry to say that in our pain we did some severing of our own.

Burying this ax, this hatchet, would mean we don't use it to sever the ties anymore. To bury that which disconnects and divides is not a denial of the pain it has caused. We must face it and feel it to heal it. There are no two ways around that. Burying is not a denial, but a decision. A decision against division.

What if we were to give the hatchet to our brothers and sisters through whom we experienced harm? Surrender it right over? What if we released the hatchet to them before placing it in the earth, allowing that which holds the power to destroy and divide to begin to disintegrate and dissolve?

There is a cemetery lining the property on which we live (how handy!). A cemetery over which others have prayed and prophesied. Numerous ones have told of seeing glory streaming down on that very site. I'm beginning to wonder if it's related to that which we could bury and the blessing it would bring.

"How very good and pleasant it is when kindred live together in unity!" the psalmist wrote. This harmony "is like the dew of Hermon, which falls on the mountains of Zion. For there the Lord ordained his blessing, life forevermore" (Psalm 133).

The words come to me now — from harm to harmony.

My husband and I have been trying to leave home for four years now. But maybe it's not our home that needs to be left. Maybe it's the hatchet we've been holding. It's hard to heal when you're holding a hatchet.

Jenny Gehman is a freelance writer, retreat speaker, and spiritual director who publishes a weekly devotional, Little Life Words, at jennygehman.com. She and her husband Dan live in Lancaster, PA where they enjoy hosting friends and strangers from around the world.

Reprinted with permission from Anabaptist World magazine, AnabaptistWorld.org.

"The Body Broken"

by Kristal Hang Calkins

I have always been confident in my body.
But when strangers tell me I look like I'm a teenager
In a way meant to sound envious,
When the Chinese Sook Sook asks me where my parents are
When I am the speaker at his church that day,
When men's glances linger on me
as they cross the street in my direction,
When older white men talk to me on the bus
Even while I have my headphones on,
When I read about a white man
killing Korean and Chinese women in a spa
to get rid of the objects of his sin,
I start to second guess myself.
The narrative I've heard is that my body is for Shame--
Even from within I am told:
"You are too skinny," but also:
"Your face is too fat, and so is your belly"
"Don't eat too much, you'll get too fat"
"Don't show too much skin, you'll distract the boys"
But also: "Flaunt your body while you're young," and
"You'll never look this good again."
It is all too much of
Never good enough.
But then I see you on that tree:
The crown of thorns upon your head
The nail pierced hands
The blood sputtering out from your side—

"This is the body

Broken for you," and also,

"Father forgive them

For they know not what they do."

In three days' time you rose from the dead,

Your body made perfect

As you showed Thomas the holes in your hands.

My Lord and my God!

They had meant your body for shame

But all along, you had meant it for Glory.

In the beginning, you created man and woman

Intending bodies for beauty—

To bear your image and abide with you,

naked and without any shame.

Instead of "never good enough"

You said "very good."

We may have fallen along the way

But you, O Bread of Life, bring redemption

Through the breaking of

Your own body, And soon, you will transform our bodies

To be glorious like yours.

Kristal is the daughter of immigrants from the Canton province of China and from Macau. When she is not giving her attention to her 5-year-old boy or newborn daughter, she enjoys reading feel-good YA novels, watching K-dramas, and sharing about what she and her kids are reading on her bookstagram (@the.curated.bookshelf).

"Faith and Felony"

by Sonia Frontera

It was one of those delicious Saturday mornings. Not an item on my agenda, I savored a quiet cup of coffee in the Silence, communing with God without a worry in the world.

Little did I know that God had plans to shake up my world. Plans to reveal his grace in unexpected ways.

A phone ring interrupted my reverie. Persistent and urgent, the ring raptured me away from my blissful contemplation.

A number from Bolivia appeared on my cell phone's screen. "Who could be calling from Bolivia?" I wondered.

"Sonia, this is Pablo," said a voice reeking of desperation and angst. I was surprised. I had never given him my phone number.

"Have you talked to Jason?" Pablo asked. "I haven't heard from him since Thursday and in the ten years we've been together he's never missed a day. I have a premonition that something terrible happened to him."

Jason was a friend from church. For years, he volunteered his time, always willing to jump in and clean the church, take out the garbage, run errands for the priest.

Jason was adored by everyone in town. He was the kind of guy who'd bring in your groceries, help you with your yard work or surprise you with a piece of homemade bread pudding. Jason boasted about the many folks who called him "my brother."

Jason and Pablo had been involved in what I believed to be a monogamous long-distance relationship. They Skyped daily, and I had witnessed countless of their calls.

But the men had never met in person. Even though I am no stranger to long-distance relationships, this arrangement baffled me. How can you commit your life to someone you've never seen?

But who am I to judge?

Just days earlier, Jason announced that Pablo was coming to the United States in the fall and that they were planning to get married. He asked me to officiate their union and, in spite of my misgivings, I agreed.

"Jason calls me every night before going to sleep," Pablo insisted. "It is not like him to miss a call, let alone two."

"It's probably nothing," I said, feigning reassurance. "He probably had to work a double and fell asleep. I will get a hold of him for you," I promised.

Jason's full mailbox answered my call, and I agonized conjuring up every conceivable tragedy that could have befallen him. Where was he? Why didn't he answer? Did he have another heart attack and was lying alone in a hospital bed? Was he even alive?

I remembered I had the phone number of one of his coworkers.

"Is Jason at work?" I texted.

"Jason won't be coming back to work anytime soon," Joel quickly replied.

"What do you mean?" I persisted, intrigued.

What I saw left me speechless. In Joel's next text, a link to a mysterious law enforcement site displayed Jason's mugshot. He had been taken into custody, accused of a crime of moral turpitude.

While Pablo anxiously awaited the call of his beloved Friday night, Jason sat in his car, anticipating an illicit sexual encounter with a random stranger in a parking lot.

The police writeup described a vigilante operation that lured Jason into a rendezvous with a fictitious young man with the mutual exchange of sexually explicit text messages and photos.

And Jason admitted to the police his role in the hookup.

"This can't be real," I told myself. "This must be a sick joke."

It wasn't. My friend, someone I loved and trusted, lived a dark secret life I knew nothing about. I was overcome by shock, anger, disgust, and disbelief.

"How could anyone be so stupid? How can you throw your life down the toilet like that?"

I reproached.

This legal fiasco meant the end of a good job where Jason was loved and respected. The demise of a long-term relationship he claimed meant the world to him. "How do I tell Pablo?" I tormented myself.

Back in the Silence, as I processed the news not knowing what to do, the words of the Master flashed through my mind, "I was in prison and you came to see me."

I felt the call of the Lord to spring into action. My friend was in trouble and God was counting on me to help.

I realized that, like judgment, forgiveness and redemption were God's business, not mine.

Notwithstanding Jason's actions, God called me to rescue a soul in peril—possibly facing death. Afflicted with depression and heart disease, I feared for Jason's life. And it is no secret that inmates facing similar charges often take their own lives.

This burden was more than I could face alone. It would take a team to unravel this mess.

Yet, I feared being judged. Judged for lending a hand to someone whose behaviors were abominable and universally condemned.

What if they repudiated Jason—or worse—repudiated me by association?

But I could not refuse. God called me to compassion, and I reached out for help.

What happened next astounded me.

God revealed that he didn't just call me to compassion. We are all called to respond to his commandment to love neighbor as the self. And to my delighted amazement, I was not the only one to say yes. A loving team assembled before my eyes.

First Elaine, a retired cop, helped me understand what Jason was up against. She told me where he was probably detained and guided me to the next steps.

"And if you want to do something nice for him, deposit money in his commissary account," she counseled. "So sorry to hear about Jason. He's such a nice guy."

Next, I summoned the troops from the church to which he devoted his life. Jason was depressed and alone in prison. Michelle and her husband rushed to the jail on Sunday morning to find out where he was imprisoned and contacted a pastor to visit him in jail.

Even though we were not permitted to visit, Jason would know his friends cared.

I had entered the judgment-free zone. I felt relieved, although briefly.

The weeks that followed knocked me with anguish and helplessness.

For the first ten days following the arrest, nobody had heard from Jason. Nobody knew if he was well. Those who loved him feared that the three kittens that were his life languished alone in his apartment without food or water. Nobody knew if they were alive or how to get them to safety. Nobody even knew his address.

My attempts to find Jason failed, until it occurred to me to leave a message with the public defender.

Hours later, Jason finally emerged, calling me from his attorney's office. He was healthy.

He was treated well. He already had friends in prison. Above all, Jason was at peace. He accepted responsibility for his mistakes and was willing to pay the price for them. "Please ask Pablo to forgive me," he exclaimed in tears. A tearful Pablo accepted the apology, grateful to hear his wayward partner was okay.

God had revealed himself again. He reminded me that redemption was his business.

My only assignment was to Love.

And God taught me that Love was not assigned to me exclusively. Love was everyone's assignment.

And as God would have it, Love prevailed.

Rescuing the kitties out of the apartment was a labor of Love. Convening five people at Jason's apartment and bringing three scared cats out of hiding was an uphill battle. But we managed to save the cats and Jason's most precious possessions. In harmony. In Love.

The building manager, the super, the friends. We worked as a team, inspired by Love, in the judgment-free zone.

Back in town, I dreaded the neighbors' interrogations. Word traveled fast and everybody knew.

Those who cherished Jason asked me about him. With Love. Without judgment.

Jason was seen through the eyes of Love as a fallen angel. As a being of Love who had poured himself out while he secretly battled invisible demons we couldn't protect him from.

The judgment-free zone got bigger and bigger.

Grace was at work.

The greatest lesson from this experience is the realization that we are all instruments of God's mercy and grace.

Grace expresses God's Love through us, as us.

If only we could extend the same grace to everyone we encounter, beholding them as holy expressions of the Christ, we could make this a just and peaceful world.

Because there is only one Christ. And we are all one with him.

It is easy to see Christ in the saints and in those who suffer. Sadly, it's harder to see Christ in the criminal, in the deviant.

But Love is more powerful than sin.

Love transforms what we behold with the eyes of the soul.
Love helps us see the Christ in the pervert, in the death-row inmate.
Love allows justice and grace to coexist. God's redemption paves the way.

Jason will atone for his deeds. He will do time in jail, and when he gets out, will forfeit the life he had envisioned for himself. He accepts it. Justice will be served.

As for Pablo, he will move on to other relationships, wiser, I hope, than before. God invites us all to co-create a just and peaceful world, one act of grace at a time. With Love, one person at a time.

Are you in?

Sonia Frontera is a contemplative, empowerment trainer and author. Her writing invites readers to discover paths to spirituality in everyday situations and personal adversity.

"Let Us Now Lament"

by Mari Fitz-Wynn

Tears flow from our prayers,
repentance bows our head.
Our ears are dulled to cries for mercy.
We've winked at injustice,
turned our face from truth
and wrongly ignored strife.
Our souls' weariness becomes
the goad by which we now come
with sins piled higher than our heads.
We lift our hands yet higher to receive
that which we've often withheld:
forgiveness, grace and peace.
Let now our lament fill the heavens

Mari Fitz-Wynn is an author, poet, and speaker. She is the founder of Faith Journey Publishing, a small press for female writers of color over the age of forty-five.

"Fearfully and Wonderfully Made"

by Mari Fitz-Wynn

I am fearfully and wonderfully made.
Long, short, kinky, curly hair for wonder's sake:

I am fearfully and wonderfully made.
Straight, flat, wide nose for freedom's fragrance:

I am fearfully and wonderfully made.
Thick, round, full, thin lips for words of hope:

I am fearfully and wonderfully made.
Big, piercing, gentle, curious eyes for searching out truth:

I am fearfully and wonderfully made.
Fisted, open, praying, reaching hands for grasping grace:

I am fearfully and wonderfully made.
Walking, running, protesting, standing on strong legs for justice:

I am fearfully and wonderfully made.
Beaten, broken bodies surviving for greater things:

I am fearfully and wonderfully made.
Gifted, challenged, curious, inspired minds set for eternity:

We are fearfully and wonderfully made.
Psalm 139:14

Mari Fitz-Wynn is an author, poet, and speaker. She is the founder of Faith Journey Publishing, a small press for female writers of color over the age of forty-five.

"Unholiday-Like"

by Margaret Bacon

She adjusted her mask as she moved forward to a marked spot in front of the grocery store. Brooke tried to ignore the stupidity she felt for shopping on the evening before Thanksgiving. Not that she was shopping for the feast. Three years ago, she'd participated in the First Nation's observance on Alcatraz and no longer acknowledged the myth that was Thanksgiving. But this year, there would be no sunrise service to mark her non-participation of a holiday based on genocide. The reason she now waited in the damp fog was that she'd put off shopping for so long that she didn't even have oat milk for her coffee, let alone coffee. She could have used a delivery service, but she felt the need to actually see what she chose to eat, and shopping gave her a reason to leave her apartment for the first time in two days.

When she finally made it to the front of the line, the security guard pointed to the hand sanitizer before she could take a basket. Brooke chose a hand basket to keep her from buying more than she could lug home on the bus and up the four flights of stairs to her studio apartment. When she first moved in, she found the old building quaint, but climbing stairs several times a day because there was no elevator had soon lost its charm.

At least with the imposed limitation of shoppers, the store wasn't overly crowded, but it was still a small grocery store with narrow aisles compared to the mega supermarkets in the suburbs. Whenever she visited her parents, she marveled at how many big chain grocery stores there were and how they always seemed empty compared to those in the city.

As she expected, when she first explained to her family that she no longer observed Thanksgiving, they'd been perplexed. In some ways, it was easier though. Her parents' divorce had always presented the awkward dilemma over whom to visit. Still, she'd assured her mother that she'd spend Christmas with her. (And the New Year being the more important holiday in Japanese tradition, she'd celebrate with her father.) This year though, even those gatherings were off. She wouldn't be celebrating with any family this season.

Such musings were not helping her already glum mood, so Brooke grabbed a basket and headed straight for the coffee aisle where she chose the darkest roast, already ground. She found her oat milk among the other milk alternative, though she still chose real cheese from the dairy section. *Just can't do vegan cheese,* she consoled herself. She picked up peanut butter and apricot jam, then strode over to produce, figuring she'd better have something fresh. She got a bag of salad mix, a small acorn squash, and three fuyu persimmons - the hard kind, not the pucker-inducing soft ones. Her family, even her *haikujin* mother, referred to the fruit as *kaki*. Reasoning that carbs were comforting, she picked up a loaf of wheat bread and a baguette to eat right away. She also treated herself to sugar cookies, even with all the additives. Brooke felt uplifted that she was done and made a beeline for the checkout. She was almost home free when the girl approached her hesitantly.

"Excuse me."

Brooke looked to the preteen who was with a younger girl and a woman, obviously her sister and mother. They were all wearing disposable masks. Brooke knew they'd approached her because she was Asian, like them. Somehow, even with her nose and mouth half covered, her hat pulled down to her glasses, they'd recognized her. Brooke stopped and acknowledged them politely though she glanced in the direction of the checkout.

"Is this alright for pumpkin pie?" the girl asked, holding up a graham cracker crust pie pan.

"Oh, no." Brooke shook her head as all three waited on her every word with wide eyes. "You need plain crust. It's in frozen foods." Trying not to sigh too loudly, she added, "I'll show you," and led the way to the freezer section. The family followed as she cruised the airtight doors until she found the frozen crusts encased in aluminum pie pans.

"Here they are," she reached in and pulled out a pair of pans. "They come in twos. You can make two pies."

"Two?" the elder girl asked. Her younger sister smiled brightly while their mother looked bewildered.

"Yeah, I'm not sure why there's two. I guess so you can make pumpkin pie and another kind, like pecan or apple…"

A tiny, elderly woman remarked in passing, "My favorite is pecan pie. I grew up in Georgia. It was never Thanksgiving without a pecan pie…" She shuffled slowly along, leaning on her cart for support.

Brooke saw that the woman's cart contained a single frozen turkey dinner. "Pecan's good!" she called after the woman, then muttered to the family, "It's also more work."

All three stared at her blankly. "You can also just keep the other crust frozen until you make another pie… for like Christmas," Brooke told them.

The family smiled at her through their masks. Brooke felt her opportunity for a quick checkout fading. "Your first time cooking Thanksgiving dinner?" she asked the obvious.

They nodded in unison. "Every year we have big family dinner," the mother spoke for the first time, haltingly. Her accent was thick. "But this year…" she shrugged. "My girls want real Thanksgiving."

Brooke could see the mother took pride in her American daughters. Despite the reference to the cringe-worthy holiday, Brooke felt herself endeared. Their cart was laden with a small frozen turkey, canned gravy, canned pumpkin pie mix, eggs, butter, and assorted fresh vegetables.

"But, what about whip cream for the pie?" the younger daughter, feeling emboldened, asked.

"Sure," Brooke agreed. "You gotta have whipped cream with pumpkin pie," she said, heading back to the dairy section. "Actually, whipped cream goes with anything, even though I try not to do cow's milk…" She stopped herself. Too much information.

In front of the refrigerated doors, Brooke pointed to the cartons of heavy whipping cream and explained, "you can whip your own or…" She pulled out a can of ready-whipped cream. "This one you just squirt." Brooke threw back her head and pantomimed squeezing cream into her mouth. They all laughed and a young black man passing by gave her a thumbs up.

"That's the one they had at winter day camp last year!" the younger daughter exclaimed. Then, her elation faded. "There's no winter camp this year. We didn't have summer camp either."

Brooke nodded. "Yeah, it's been a hell of a year." She looked to mother to see if she'd used inappropriate language, but the family all just nodded in agreement.

"You're gonna need this little sister." Brooke handed the can to the younger girl who happily added it to their cart.

"Thank you," the mother said. She reached out and touched Brooke on the arm. Then, as if remembering, she drew back and bowed slightly. The girls chorused their appreciation.

"Of course!" Brooke bowed slightly back.

As they headed to the checkout together Brooke said, "So I guess you better thaw that bird right away. Are you going to stuff it?"

Again, they all looked doubtful. Brooke silently admonished herself. "Usually, there's dressing with turkey," she explained. "Most people do bread, but my family always stuffed the bird with rice."

"I cook rice," mother said.

"But the American one is bread, right?" the elder daughter asked. "Do we have to stuff?"

They all looked worried.

"No. In fact, the turkey cooks faster without stuffing and it's actually safer to make the dressing on the side" Brooke informed them. It was beginning to surprise her how much she knew for never having cooked a Thanksgiving dinner by herself. She spun around and, with the family on her heels, found the Thanksgiving section where she picked up a box of stuffing mix.

"Here," she handed it to the elder daughter. "The instructions on how to cook it on the stove or in the oven are on the box." She was starting to feel a little guilty for introducing the family to so much processed food. She could only console herself that canned and boxed food was part of an all-American experience and hopefully they didn't eat sugar, salt, and preservatives often.

"Oh, thank God!" A tall, thin man with a bandana joined them at the Thanksgiving display and began piling canned sweet potatoes into his basket. Even through her mask Brooke picked up the strong scent of cannabis. "Last year, they ran out of sweet potatoes *and* marshmallows!" He grabbed a bag of the fluffy confections. "What are the marshmallows for?" the younger daughter asked Brooke, but the man answered.

"They go on top of the sweet potatoes. My roommates would kill me if I forgot the marshmallows! It like makes the dish!"

Behind him Brooke frowned and shook her head. The family laughed aloud, but the man was oblivious and ran off.

"We don't have sweet potatoes." The elder daughter looked concerned.

"Well," Brooke sighed. "If you're going to do sweet potatoes, I say do them fresh. It's real easy. You just peel 'em, slice 'em, and roast until soft, then smother with butter, syrup, and cinnamon. I mean, you can get real fancy…" She stopped as the three stared at her.

"We have pancake syrup," the younger daughter offered.

"That'll work," Brooke shrugged and led them to the produce section.

"Oh, so many kind!" The mother exclaimed, looking at the assortment of sweet potatoes, and yams, including purple varieties.

"Yeah," Brooke nodded. "I didn't know they had Japanese sweet potato!"

"That is *ube*," a middle-aged woman corrected her. "It is Filipino."

Brooke was about to ask how she knew, but simply shrugged. "Still delicious and so pretty!"

The woman gave her a knowing look and filled her plastic bag with *ube*. Brooke placed one in her own basket while the family looked on.

"Which is the American one?" the elder daughter asked.

"I guess the orange sweet potato," Brooke answered.

"How many?" The mother asked.

"How many in your family?"

"Just us… and our father," the elder daughter told her.

"How about five then… one each and an extra."

The mother took care choosing each potato and Brooke waited patiently with them. Finally, they walked back to the checkout where the line had grown. The elder sister was studying the stuffing box while her younger sister bounced up and down gleefully. Their mother smiled through her mask watching her daughters.

"What do you usually have for Thanksgiving?" Brooke asked the younger daughter.

"Chinese food," she answered. "Everyone brings something they cooked, but my mother, sister, and I always make the pots stickers."

"You make your own pot stickers?!"

The mother nodded enthusiastically.

"My grandmother made pot stickers… we call them *gyoza*," Brooke recalled fondly. Even though she no longer ate meat, the pork dumplings had been a favorite when she was a child.

The elder daughter looked up from the stuffing box. "Oh *gyoza*. You're Japanese."

"Yeah, well Japanese American. My great grandparents on my father's side were from Japan."

"You always celebrated Thanksgiving, American style?" Th elder daughter asked.

Brooke nodded sheepishly. "Yes, with my family. Not anymore though…" She wasn't sure how to explain her recent anti-Thanksgiving stance, so she said nothing more. The family looked at her sadly and she knew they were thinking she couldn't celebrate because of the pandemic.

Brooke checked out first and turned to say goodbye. She realized she'd become fond of the family, so she grabbed a pen from her purse and made a motion to ask if it was okay to write on one of their plastic shopping bags. They all nodded. She scribbled her name and number telling them, "If you have any questions, feel free to call. I'm not much of a cook, but…"

The elder daughter looked at the writing and read out loud, "Brooke."

"That's me!" she said before starting off. "It's been nice talking to you."

"Happy Thanksgiving!" they all called after her.

Brooke winced but turned back and waved with a smile.

Outside it was dark and she had to wait longer than usual for the bus. Like everything, the schedules had all been adjusted. Once home, Brooke picked up her mail, climbed the stairs, and let herself into her apartment. As she unloaded the groceries in her kitchenette, she realized she had all the fixings for a vegan Thanksgiving dinner, the sides anyway. Despite her new aversion to the holiday, she had to admit that she'd missed the meal. She even liked turkey though she no longer ate the poor bird, bred for as much breast meat as possible so that it could hardly stand up.

After setting the kettle on the stove for a cup of tea, she sank into one of the two deep armchairs that made up her living room. She took comfort in the musty smell of the heater cranking up. The mail she'd thrown on the side table caught her eye and she picked up an orange envelope that she knew right away was from her mother. Though the card had an autumn motif of colorful fall leaves and pumpkins, there was no reference to the holiday. Neither inside was there a sappy sentiment, just her mother's familiar cursive, telling her daughter that she loved her and missed her. Brooke wiped away the first tear that ran down her cheek, then she let them flow, relishing the comfort of a good cry.

When her phone rang, Brooke answered it with a sniffle. Even though she didn't recognize the number, she knew the voice. "Hello Brooke, how do we defrost the turkey?"

THE END

Margaret Bacon is a Hapa writer of Okinawan and Anglo American descent. She has been a freelance writer most of her life and has one book of fiction, Yuletide Angels *with eLectio Publishing.*

"Heal"

by Ike Sturm

Heal

recklessly we climb
above the blue-green labyrinth
pushing beyond our limits
magnetic beings etching
divisions with a razor's edge

must I take this dive
or might I take a breath
now and then again
each pause a parachute
enlightening us down to our feet

no one knows the hurt
the aches that built your heart
but I see the way you dig
and listen and pray
listening from the inside

the spark of your spirit
stokes the ancient blaze of your eyes
among the Beloved's great works
is the curious joy you radiate
like love waves around the world

Community whisperer, bassist, composer, Ike Sturm lives in the Hudson Valley and knits a connect.faith program called Finding Our Way Home. He also plays around the world in one-half of the environmentally-minded duo, Endless Field.

"Finding Hope Among the Hopeless"

by Jean P. Kelly

In an "oasis of joy" established by Dorothy Day, I realized I was not only a helper but also the helped.

I heard him before I saw him. A disembodied, but plaintive voice intoned from somewhere on the second deck of the Staten Island Ferry, saying "I just visited my aunt, but she wasn't home. I'm homeless. Someone stole all my things. I was stupid. I thought I could handle drugs. I couldn't, but I've been clean 6 months. I need seven dollars to shower and get something to eat."

A waifish man, half-hidden under a red hoody, rounded the corner and came nearer. He politely repeated his refrain, adding "I am Phillip. Like many 20-year-olds, I had a problem with drugs, but I have been clean 6 months."

He made a circuit of every level, both exterior and interior decks, hands out, weeping and apologizing for his emotional appeal. Streetwise New Yorkers avoided eye contact. One woman handed him two dollars. I hesitated, but then decided my moral code favored generosity over judgment, trust over scrutiny. I dug out what little cash I carried, put it in his palm, and he continued along his way.

On the port side the ferry passed the Statue of Liberty lifting her torch above a cold, dreary harbor. I couldn't help but find ironic that the "Mother of Exiles" looked down upon her own people who were "huddled masses yearning to be free," of poverty, addiction and indifference. Her lamp revealed a desperately divided and distracted nation. But I refused to be discouraged. I was in the city retracing the steps of my progressive Christian heroine and fellow journalist, Dorothy Day. In 1933, she established a newspaper and a movement or "for those who are huddling in shelters trying to escape the rain, for those who are walking the streets in the all but futile search for work, for those who think that there is no hope for the future, no recognition of their plight." Her homeless shelters and Catholic Worker organizations, both in New York and across the country, are still going strong today. I had come from Ohio to work for a week in the places Day called "houses of hospitality" for the marginalized she called "guests."

I have a poster of Day in my office, where it serves as inspiration for my work empowering college students to take social action as part of their college program and, I hope, their future after graduation. "We can to a certain extent change the world," it says, quoting her. "We can work for the oasis, the little cell of joy and peace in a harried world. We can throw our pebble in the pond and be confident that its ever-widening circle will reach around the world."

More than eight decades after she sold her first newspaper for a penny and started a movement, Catholic Workers continue to change the world. During my stay on the Lower East Side, I found each, one for men and one for women, to be oases of joy, peace, and perhaps what I most needed, hope.

I had visited Day's grave on Staten Island and where she once owned a cabin there and was returning to Manhattan. After the ferry docked, I was swept along with the terminal crowd, until I found a spot on a standing-room-only subway car on its way to Chelsea where I intended to do some sightseeing. I snatch an overhead strap just as the train lurched forward, then gladly took a seat offered by a male passenger. Then I heard a nearby voice say quietly, "I'm sorry m'am that I didn't get up. I didn't see you."

Without looking in the direction of the speaker, I reflexively responded, "That's okay."

Then I recognized the soft-spoken politeness.

"You are Phillip, from the ferry!" I exclaimed. He looked over at me in the next seat and smiled. His teeth were jagged, black, and some were missing all together. I knew a meth-mouth when I saw it, dentition ground to nubs during highs on methamphetamines. Because I had already been working in the shelters for a few days, I asked if Phillip had asked for help at one, St. Joseph's.

He grinned: "The guys there are like family to me," he said. "Jim, Carmen.

"I can tell you I would not be sober at all were it not for them."

Addiction had numbed his emotions, he went on to tell me, but his ability to be grateful was growing, thanks to treatment in a recovery center near St Joseph's.

While I'm unsure even now why I felt a connection to this total stranger, whether it was his vulnerability or my own, soon I was spilling out my own story. I had just ended a long marriage to an addict, I confessed, a binge alcoholic. I was on this trip in search of a new direction, though I wasn't quite sure where I should turn next.

Phillip followed with a barrage of questions, and I felt relieved to be able to provide honest answers. Was my husband still drinking? Yes. Was he abusive? Psychologically, yes. Physically? Yes. Had he moved out? No, he refused to leave our family's home. Did I have children? Yes, three teen daughters.

Too soon brakes screeched and Phillip stood. He inclined his hooded head toward mine and asked, again, for my name. I replied and promised to tell the staff at St. Joseph's we had met. Then, as the train doors opened, familiar words crossed my lips, but for perhaps the first time, they sounded sincere to my ears: "I will pray for you," I promised as he exited. "Thank you," he mouthed back to me.

Dorothy Day was no stranger to addicts like Phillip. Whether she met them in prison while serving time for civil disobedience or whether she caroused alongside them as friends, the artists, activists, and anarchists of 1920-era Greenwich Village. Though never addicted herself, she seem to possess an intense empathy for those who dull pain with addictive substances. In one autobiography she wrote, "I was that drug addict, screaming and tossing in her cell, beating her head against the wall.…The blackness of hell was all about me. The sorrows of the world encompassed me. I was like one gone down into the pit. Hope had forsaken me."

Day did, in her early life, suffer the consequences of disconsolate lifestyle: a pregnancy that ended in abortion, two suicide attempts, and a divorce from a man she married on a rebound. After late nights with her friends, however, she began to seek solace in the pews of open Catholic churches near the Village. At dawn Masses, she'd sit "in the back …not knowing what was going on at the altar, but warmed and comforted by the lights and silence, the kneeling people," she later wrote. "People have so great a need to reverence, to adore; it is a psychological necessity of human nature."

Day subsequently pursued her curiosity about faith with an impassioned singularity. "I wanted to be poor, chaste, and obedient," she wrote in *The Long Loneliness*. "I wanted to die in order to live, to put off the old man and put on Christ." Day became Catholic in December 1927, just a few months after she baptized her only child, Tamar Teresa, into the same church. She raised her daughter alone and never married, because the child's father did not support her conversion.

While working at Maryhouse, the woman's shelter where Day lived until her death in 1980, I was thrilled to meet Tamar's daughter, Martha Hennessey. She characterized her grandmother's faith as so fierce it was frightening. "I remember sitting on her lap and having my ear on her chest. That was the first time I understood God: the mystery of God was Granny's heart."

That fierceness of faith is perhaps why Day's legacy, especially her militantly egalitarian philosophies, appear to be completely unchanged as practiced by Catholic Workers today. Never before, not in thirty years of work in homeless agencies as a volunteer, board member and leader, had I witnessed such dignity and mutual respect in the relationship between the helpers and the helped as I did that week. At St. Joseph's, the soup, bread and coffee were served to guests at tables, restaurant-style. When a father and son arrived after lunch was put away, they were offered not a few slices of bread, but rather an entire loaf and a full jar of peanut butter, no questions asked. At the clothing room in the women's facility, guests could try items on, making sure donated items fit both their bodies and their sense of style, just as they might in Midtown.

Catholic Workers, many of whom take a voluntary vow of poverty to live at the shelters, are likewise clothed in donated items, which is why I sometimes struggled to distinguish between the helpers and the helped. Once two women in the soup line danced to music playing on a cell phone. Not until the older of the two rushed to aid a guest collapsed on the sidewalk outside--due to dehydration and hunger--did I learn she was a retired public health nurse and a volunteer. The woman playing funk on her phone was there to be fed.

At St. Joseph's I watched a pair of thirty-something men, each dressed entirely in black, deep in conversation after lunch, heads together. One man was slight and bespectacled. The other was long-legged, with a square jaw and deep eyes peeking from beneath a black knit cap. He reminded me of my handsome oldest nephew and looked about the same age. Not until this man stood, picked up a suitcase near his chair, and walked back into the street, did I realize who was who. It turned out the smaller man was a seminarian, ministering to the lost, the addicted, and forgotten by simply being present to them. The taller was like my brother's oldest son, an addict. Though my nephew was never materially poor, he struggled with mental illness and poverty of spirit until he died at age 40. Tragically, by then, he was more alone than the young man at the shelter that day.

"Those who cannot see the face of Christ in the poor," Day used to say, "are atheists indeed."

Perhaps it is no surprise that after Day's death in 2002, a movement started to recognize her as a saint. Catholics believe that any soul rewarded by seeing Christ's face in heaven is a saint, but the Church also researches particularly holy people to see if their lives on earth, miracles credited to them after death, and devotion by those who pray to them raises them to the lexicon of named saints. Day's "cause" has progressed through some of the sainthood stages, with the church bestowing upon her the title "Servant of God."

Whether it is appropriate for Day to become a saint, however, remains a matter of some debate. During her life, she was as likely to pray for the intercession of Gandhi as she was to call out to St. Francis or the Virgin Mary. Some considered her a heretic, a secret Communist, or even "loathsome," according to a state senator from Virginia who wrote to Pope Benedict in opposition to her cause. A quick Google search of her name and the keyword "saint" is sure to uncover results referring to her famous statement that seems to mock sainthood. "Don't call me a saint," she once said. "I don't want to be dismissed that easily."

"She worried that people would put her up on a pedestal, that they would believe her to be without faults," wrote her friend Robert Ellsberg in a *Catholic Worker* newspaper column in 2015. She was not uninterested in sainthood, he wrote, but "she felt this was a way for people to dismiss her witness and let *themselves* off the hook."

Day sincerely believed it was possible to live as saints in modern times. "We are all called to be saints, and we might as well get over our bourgeois fear of the name. We might also get used to recognizing the fact that there is some of the saint in all of us."

That saintliness is why Catholic Workers, then and now, never give up on the recalcitrant, even when there is "no chance of rehabilitation, no chance, so far as we see, of changing them," she wrote. She called all Christians to holiness by retaining hope and having mercy even for the hopeless.

Near the end of my week as a volunteer, I had a chance to share my story about Phillip with Carmen Trotta, a long-time St. Joseph staffer who worked with Dorothy Day. He looked puzzled. I added details.

"He said he's been clean six months, that he is being treated at a rehab center near here. Lanky kid."

"With the horrible teeth?" Trotta asked.

Yes, I said.

"He told you he's been clean 6 months? More likely 6 hours," Trotta explained impatiently. "I'll be surprised if he is still alive next week."

I was crest-fallen, not to mentioned demurred by my obvious naivete. Though sincere, I realized how little I understood about day-to-day realities of life in the Bowery. I didn't fault Trotta for his obvious frustration with a day-tripping do-gooder like me. As one Catholic Worker explained, those who fight so long and so hard against trenchant injustice rarely have patience for those who do not get it. "We do nice things," he said, "but we are not nice people."

Perhaps not, but the attractiveness of the oasis created by the fiercely faithful was difficult to resist. After several weeks at home in Ohio, no longer a place of peace and joy if it ever was, I was back in New York at St Joseph's. This time I brought two of my daughters. From the time they were barely tall enough to see over a kitchen counter to then, they worked alongside me in breadlines and soup kitchens. They easily took to the routine of serving what seemed like a never-ending line of guests that day.

My youngest wiped down tables once the meal was finished, her sister picked up trash, and I walked toward the refrigerator with plates of butter that could be served again the next day. Near the coffeemaker, I noticed a thin man with his back to me. He had missed the meal, so was instead filling a Styrofoam cup with liquid to warm him against the street's early April chill. As he turned to leave, I glimpsed a jagged tooth.

"Phillip!" I exclaimed. He immediately embraced me. I hurriedly introduced my daughters, who had heard all about him. He then asked in a whisper if their father had moved out. He had not, I replied.

Phillip energetically demonstrated what addiction therapists call "stinkin' thinking" and what I came to know as manipulative lying. He was still in rehab, he said, and still sober. I didn't argue, so positively joyful that my daily prayers on his behalf had been answered: he was still among the living, still with a chance at redemption, still with hope. I told him as much.

But then he trumped me. "I have been praying for you, too," he said. "For your daughters. For your family."

A Catholic Worker then hustled Phillip toward the door so clean-up could be completed. My daughters waved at him and I said a quick goodbye, pausing to watch him return to the streets and an uncertain future. I was no longer naïve enough to think I'd see him again. I was just grateful for our two encounters, along with the grace that brought us together in the first place, when we both needed hope.

As my daughters and I departed St. Joseph's, I recalled how, in 1946, Dorothy Day ended her weekly column "On Pilgrimage" with a prayer she wrote in honor of Christmas. Her words resonate as perhaps the best possible reason to hold onto hope, especially for the Phillips of the world: love.

"There is nothing that we can do but love.
Dear God—please enlarge our hearts to love each other,
to love our neighbor,
to love our enemy as well as our friend."
Amen.

Jean P. Kelly believes in the power of stories, both hers and others, to give hope, build faith, and improve communities. Over the last 30 years, her essays and feature articles have been published in local, regional and national publications and websites. She regularly contributes essays, cultural commentary, and stories to both the online and print edition of U.S. Catholic. She often explores in her work the intersections of faith, intellect, and writing and reading as forms of prayer. Follow Jean at www.jeanpkelly.com.

"Humbly Human...And Holy"

by Karen Wicker

I was savoring every moment of an overnight retreat with my friend, Nancy. We were inspired, comforted, and challenged as we learned about *Boundless Compassion* during our time together, based on Joyce Rupp's beautiful book with the same title.

Taking time away for quiet contemplation helps open our souls to the movement of the Spirit. During one break, I sat at the small lake, pondering an insight we had just discussed. In her book, Joyce Rupp writes, *"Research by quantum physicists like David Bohm assures us that we are also united on a physical plane by a bond of invisible connections. Our physical self consists of invisible energy packets of light and heat called photons... every particle is in motion. Each part connects and interrelates with each other."*[1]

Isn't this discovery SO miraculous and delightful? The Light of God's goodness and love pervades every part of God's creation!

I began to sense that I too, was divinely connected to God, to Christ, to all of humanity, and to the entire universe. This idea of infinite connection - along with the wonder and serenity of the moment - overwhelmed me with joy and tenderness. I went back inside for the next session, feeling grateful, loved, and holy.

Sr. Dean had just begun introducing the next session when I was surprised by another sudden thought: *Yes, Karen, you are divinely connected to God and the universe. You are part of God's infinite light and love; you are intertwined with all of life.*

You are also connected to the toad, the snake, and the slug.

I almost laughed aloud! It seemed as if God was reminding me that I am still a lowly human. I may soar with the angels - but I will also slog through the mud with those I find "less lovely".

Now, as I reflect on this time, I find a greater purpose to God's marvelous photons and how they interconnect with all of creation. We are meant to be connected in love, in holy light; we have been created in love and light for this very reason! To see ourselves or any other part of creation as perfectly divine or as pitifully demeaned will only keep us prideful, judgmental, and uncaring, or envious, hopeless, and despairing. We are connected through our holiness *and* our brokenness. We need this awareness that we are both holy and broken in order to be lovingly united with all living beings.

My reflection went one step further. Too often, I come before God as more broken than beautiful. God seems to be showing me that I am equally both, and beloved as both. As God reveals my humble humanity, I am also assured that I am still a beautiful blessing...

I am broken, and I am beloved.
I am human, and I am holy.
I am insignificant, and I am immense.
I am imperfect, and I am incredible.
I am lowly, and I am lovely.

I am but a tiny flicker on the horizon... and I am also the infinite light of God.

A BENEDICTION:

May you find you are an integral part
of the infinite light of Love -
a small but essential ray of hope
to help others rise above
the darkness of their grief or pain,
the depth of their dejection.
May you be one who helps them know
we share a divine connection.

May you rejoice in every imperfection
and smile with every flaw
for you are perfectly created
by our God of wonder and awe.
May you thank God for merciful grace
as you recognize your humanity,
and share the light of God's true love
as you celebrate your divinity.

Karen Wicker is a spiritual writer who shares meditations on her blog site, https://simplysoulsearching.com. Since her time with cancer, she appreciates these bonus days to spend with family and friends, walk in nature, and write her contemplative memoir.

[1]Rupp, Joyce. *Boundless Compassion.* Notre Dame: Sorin Books; 2018: page 17.

"Feast of All Souls – Kaua'I"

by Rhonda Miska

A six-foot amazon of a native woman named Nakine - which is Hawaiian for "hope" - serves as our guide. On the van ride from Nawiliwili, she tells us to take off our jewelry, be careful of the coral, and not worry about sharks. Decked out in flippers, a snorkel mask, and the black girdle of a wetsuit, I venture into a brave new world.

The visual symphony in the coral reef of clownfish, bright-eye damselfish, angelfish. The slim, smooth, length of silver that is a needlefish. The Christmas wrasse, whose appearance is reminiscent of a holiday decoration, the practically-named rockmover, the exotic Moorish idol which does somehow evoke 13th Century Cordoba, the triggerfish with the impossibly Hawaiian name *humuhumunukunukuapua'a*. A peacock flounder, flat and mottled and perfectly matching the sea floor. Some almost comical-looking, polka dotted or 80s pop star eye shadow iridescent blue. Every possible color and pattern like a pile of disco clothes to be sorted at a thrift store. Extravagant.

My own gasp is muffled by my snorkel mouthpiece when I spot the green sea turtle. Ancient face, heart-shaped shell, with gray and brown mottling in an intricate design, and a patch of algae which will be food for a passing fish. A lovely stub of a curled-under tail. His ancestors have been in this water for 200 million years. Soaring in the sea, a winged reptilian angel. My tears behind my snorkel mask are hot in contrast to the water of the bay.

His front flipper is tangled in fishing line, impeding his silent underwater ballet, and for a moment I regret our species. I want to tell him that I'm sorry and that I love him and that we're all in this together.

I gesture to Nakine, point out the turtle's obstacle. She holds her breath, unsheathes the knife tethered to her strong, brown calf and approaches him. Maybe inherently trusting or perhaps sensing her benevolence, he extends his flipper, placid and humble. She skillfully cuts away the fishing line, like Jesus exorcising a demon, that of human arrogance and carelessness. The turtle blinks his eyes at Nakine, soundless gratitude, then with his newly liberated limb swims away like a bird flying through a summer sky, ascending.

The Talmud says to save a single life is to save the whole world. Today is the feast of all souls. *All* souls. With my own breath in my ears and a dazzling array of life displayed as far as I can see, I pray for the gift of a blade to strap to my own muscular calf, to unbind and loosen and free.

Rhonda Miska is a lay minister, preacher, poet, and spiritual director based in Minneapolis-St. Paul, MN. She has studied at the Boston College School of Theology and Ministry and the Aquinas Institute of Theology, and her past ministries include service in parishes, universities, retreat centers, social service agencies, and intentional residential communities.

"Be Like Rain"

by Jenny Gehman

My son's 12th birthday arrived on a sweltering July day. A group of us had gathered for an outdoor celebration when the thick humidity gave way to a sudden storm. Huddled together under a large tent we watched as the rain poured, the thunder roared and a bolt of lightning struck a tree across the street. We were safe, but shaken.

A few months ago my same son, 16 years later, met outdoors with a friend to catch up on their lives. The conversation turned political and a sudden storm, not unlike the birthday one, broke loose unbidden. What was to be a celebratory time of friendship turned tense as words, this time, rained down and fireballs struck close, catching my son unaware and without safe shelter.

While I typically think of rain as water falling from the skies, its definition is as broad as a large quantity of anything falling rapidly or in quick succession.

As in a rain of abuse or a shower of blessings.

What's been falling on your head of late? And to what effect, healing or harm?

"May he be like rain."

Many think David penned this prayer for his son, Solomon, at the start of his kingly reign. A father's longing laid right out, a dream and desire declared: "May he be like rain that falls on the mown grass, like showers that water the earth" (Psalm 72:6).

I've been thinking about rain. And reign. And the interplay of the two.

The classic Bible commentary by Joseph Benson tells me the rain the psalmist is praying for points to "an administration that is so gentle and easy that it will refresh and revive the hearts of its subjects and render them a flourishing people."

There is a reign/rain that renders us flourishing. How beautiful is that? And how necessary right now.

Albert Barnes' "Notes on the Whole Bible" speaks of the mown field on which this rain falls as one whose grass has been eaten off by locusts.

The idea, Barnes says, is that "after locusts have passed over a field, devouring everything, the rain descends, the fields revive and nature again puts on the appearance of life."

The past few years have left many as a devoured field. Do you feel the rawness of having been eaten down to stubble by all that has descended upon us? The fires, the fears, the fury. More than ever, we are in need of a righteous, refreshing, reviving reign/rain.

God says the words he speaks are like rain falling down (Isaiah 55:10-11).

Moses prays his teaching will fall like rain (Deuteronomy 32:2).

The prophet Joel speaks of Jesus 'teaching as "rain out of heaven, showers of words to refresh and nourish our soul" (Joel 2:23, Message).

What's falling on you? More importantly, what's falling from you?

Does it bring harm or healing?

Politicians, pastors and prophets aren't the only ones to rain down words or works. We all do. Each of us carries our own atmospheres and lets loose on those around us, not unlike my son's friend. But to what effect? Do we come down hard on others or render them a flourishing people?

Sadly, my son was on the receiving end of his friend's hailstorm, which decimated his landscape and damaged their relationship. I fear there is too much of this unleashing these days. So many sudden storms over unsuspecting people.

"He comes as rain comes," Hosea says of God, "as spring rain, refreshing the ground" (Hosea 6:3, Message).

How do you rain? How do I? Are we all thunder and lightning, unaware of the pain and fear we cause, igniting fires one after another? Or do we rain down justice, righteousness, peace and protection?

I plead for us now alongside David: May we be like rain. Gentle rain on all the raw places.

May our words and works heal, not harm. May we be good news to all on whom we fall. May we render them flourishing.

Jenny Gehman is a freelance writer, retreat speaker, and spiritual director who publishes a weekly devotional, Little Life Words, at jennygehman.com. She and her husband Dan live in Lancaster, PA where they enjoy hosting friends and strangers from around the world.

Reprinted with permission from Anabaptist World magazine, AnabaptistWorld.org. *(slight changes have been made)*

"The Heart of Resistance"

by Jason Villegas

"We're prophets of a future that is not our own,"
It seems our best times have predeceased us.
We're midwives of a promise that is still unknown.
When we talk about new life, it makes the Beast fuss.
Sometimes we fight about just when life begins
While migrants die of thirst in the Real Death Valley
They say we should keep putting wine in old wine skins,
That's the same thing that they said when slaves sat in the galley.

It's funny how El Alamo's a sign of Texas freedom,
Just down the road encroaching injustice rages
At best their souls are beaten and at worst — eaten,
You think you'd be real different if we put you into cages?
Our Lord was an immigrant whose name was Jesús,
They hated him and yet he made resistance a habit,
More times than once he avoided their noose,
with totalizing tactics that were just like Br'er Rabbit!

Jesus found a way to skip the condemnation
And set up a model for coexistence
We have an ever-changing US population,
So let's claim the Church as the heart of Resistance
You'll never know what you don't know until you give up what you
know is wrong.

When did we get hooked on the polarizing poison,
It's like we got bit by grimy snake views.
You'd think we all want reform over prison,
But sometimes we get tricked by endless fake news.
2016 was a really tough year.
The griping was like a barking Chihuahua
there were a lot of things that set free fear,
as divisive words flowed from La Casa Blanca.

"Only I can save you, and just me alone,"
We've heard claims like this and others that are *yuge*
The Devil's attack goes after our shalom,
Being shut off from others is like Ebenezer Scrooge.
When the welcome house becomes a concentration camp
It ought to be something that we all can condemn,
Nationalistic rhetoric is a population clamp,
a vice that serves to Make America Hate Again.

Somehow we've become a DomiNation.
It's time to tap into the art of persistance
We have an ever-changing US population,
So let's claim the Church as the heart of Resistance
You'll never know what you don't know until you give up what you know is wrong.

Y'all we've been here before, and God helped us through.
We can do it again, but I know it won't be pretty,
Let's give up the divisions that we know aren't true,
and begin to ignore the Back to Egypt Committee.
There are children of God who suffer family separation
Bringing them together can be a common ground

And this ain't even something that should stall with preparation, Every person that we put off is someone who might get drowned.

There's possibility now, but we gotta see the Border
The biggest problem comes when we think we are proficient,
We begin to settle in and make an immovable Order.
The greatest danger then is just that we're complacent.
We've seen a whole lot that should raise our alarm,
or at the very least get our butts off the floor.
Wesley's wisdom tells us, "Do no harm,"
And Jesus Christ says, "Go and sin no more."

It's time to wake up and resist the condemnation
Loving each other gives us a chance at existence
We have an ever-changing US population,
So let's claim the Church as the heart of Resistance.
You'll never know what you don't know until you give up what you
know is wrong.

Having been raised in multiple geographic, ethnic, and denominational spaces, Jason Villegas brings to his work an intentional position of understanding the complexities of our diverse, increasingly secular world with hopes to bridge the gaps between them. He is an ordained elder in the North Carolina Conference of the United Methodist Church, currently serving both as the Conference Director of Youth Ministry and also as a local church pastor, being half of a clergy couple with children and working to finish his doctor of ministry degree from Duke University Divinity School (spring, 2023).

"Embrace God's Sending"

by Elizabeth A. Moyer

And let us consider how to provoke one another to love and good deeds, not neglecting to meet together, as is the habit of some, but encouraging one another, and all the more as you see the Day approaching. Hebrews 10:24-25, NRSV

"Not forsaking the assembling of ourselves together" are words that have played on a loop in my head since summer 2018, the last time my family attended an in-person worship service. The words have been played on a damning damaging loop as I have struggled with the institutional church. The church has comfortably marginalized me because of gender, race, family of origin, marital status, and more. The church wherein a body of believers toss around words like "good stock" when evaluating someone's worthiness for ministry. The local fellowship whose vision seems wholly concerned about the number of people gathering instead of the number of people transformed and serving in the community. The local fellowship appears to have lost the passion of the *Missio Dei* that is the "mission of God."

Serving in pastoral leadership left me questioning the local church's mission, vision, and values. I have never been one to question individuals who say, "they do not do church" or "are not religious," I firmly believe the message of the cross calls me to meet people in the space where they are and share my life with them as well as the gospel. If my life is a testament to the One I claim to follow, it may inspire others to want to embark on their journey. Therefore, you cannot measure that sharing by the number of individuals who show up on Sunday or those who join or attend a particular fellowship.

The measure of sharing is a body of believers that serve, in the local church, the local community, and beyond, people who are actively engaged in mission because God is a sending God; people are sent. A church ripe with missional imagination committed to going into the neighborhood's discovering new ways to invite people to join in God's mission, not sit in a sanctuary.

Whether Roman Catholicism, Eastern Orthodoxy, or Protestantism, Christianity is rich in history. There is space for everyone to find their way, and the path may not lead to the branch of Christianity of the person that introduces them to the faith. The directive is to share the gospel's message, not the message of a particular church. Yet, somehow my recent experiences, the experiences that drove me to neglect the meeting together, are rooted in filling the seats of the building, not building the church, not building the people. Our denominational lines and the breaking of branches have made us enemies or frenemies within God's family.

How and why we gather are more important that where we gather. God's family can gather anywhere. I have experienced authentic worship in parks, gardens, parking lots, in unexpected places. I have experienced rote worship in some of the most adored houses of worship that money could buy. I have witnessed and been part of a tug-of-war wherein followers of Christ desire to set aside personal agendas, personal accolades, dare I say, setting aside the building fund to move beyond the walls of the building. Because sadly, many people do not always feel welcomed within our sanctuary walls.

I encourage people to explore Christianity and fall in love with Jesus, not a building, pastor, choir, or a friend that may be sitting next to you; all are temporal. I fell in love with Jesus and chose to embrace God's sending. I invite people to follow Jesus and join the communion of saints. And gather in an accepting place where growth continues. Acknowledging, the local church should be patient; we are all sinners, we are all running a race, and each individual is responsible for their pace. And commune with a body of believers living life as the hands and feet. The work of the local church happens outside of the gathering place. When I move beyond the sanctuary giving up my time, talents, and resources in my city, I become the hands and feet of Jesus, a light unto my community.

Leading in the local church complicated following Christ pushed me into the "orphaned" place of forsaking gathering together. I am a better leader because of this season; I am grateful for the season of the pandemic because it forced me to rest in the season of forsaking longer. My season of not gathering (in person at least) helped me reaffirm who I am and why I believe in the mystery of the Holy Trinity.

I know God is in the business of sending people out into the world, not recruiting more people to come to sit in pews or chairs. As many local congregations struggle with low attendance, limited funds, denominational upheaval, and so on, it may be time to embrace God's sending. Could it be that amid these struggles, God invites us to follow Christ into our communities as servants as we move beyond being keepers of empty places?

Elizabeth Moyer is a follower of Christ, wife, mom, and blogger (faryetclose.com) with a passion for community engagement and the church's missional identity. As a teacher of the faith, author, and academic researcher, she strives to inspire others to follow Christ into their communities.

"Colossus Sequel (Colossal Despair)"

by Doris Kersten

In September 2021 when news accounts told of Haitian refugees turned away at the Texas border, I again recalled the welcoming words of Emma Lazarus in her poem, "The New Colossus," provoking me to lament these recurring border tragedies as our nation still struggles to define a compassionate immigration policy.

Colossus Sequel (Colossal Despair)

Give me your tired refugees
now huddled at the border.
But don't come now; we need more time
to get our plans in order!

I'm sorry, says Miss Liberty,
we just can't take in more.
Regretfully, I dim my lamp
and close the Golden Door.

Doris lives in Westchester County, New York, and enjoys walks with friends, music, low-key yardwork, the caring community at Pleasantville Presbyterian Church, and cherished family visits with her children and grandchildren. A retired social worker and former volunteer hospital chaplain, she often turns to writing — whether poetry, letters, or journaling — for help in exploring her feelings and clarifying cares and concerns.

"The Unborn Child I Saw"

by Carol Rusaw

How do you deal with losing a child? For many, the death means a loss of memories of love, hopes for an unrealized future, and unfilled expectations of gifts, abilities, and potentials. Parents who have lost children keep treasures of stored episodes to tap in times of need. But for other parents whose children have died in utero, there are no memories. I am a childless mother who had children without giving them life. Birthing two stillborn babies and experiencing two abortions-one spontaneous and one therapeutic-profoundly changed my ideas of parenting, particularly in relationship to myself, children, and to God. I spent 40 years in a wilderness seeking resolutions. Until last year.

Mike and I decided to have children shortly after we were married. Mike especially liked having a family. His parents, like mine, had divorced and had limited contact with us. For me, having children would mean entering a new and exciting journey. I had no brothers and sisters and wondered what a real family life looked like.

Within the first year of marriage, Mike and I looked forward to our first child. I had experienced bleeding early in the pregnancy, but after some bedrest, was able to resume normal activities. The day Mike left for Vietnam, however, I began to have labor pains. I had to tell Mike we lost our son.

The doctor encouraged us to try again, since everything else was normal; we did when I was finishing a graduate degree in education. On Christmas Eve, however, I lost the second baby. This devastated us. But the doctor gave us hope when he explained that I had a double uterus that would expel fetuses as it grew. By having a surgery, the wall separating the two halves would be removed and I would be able to carry children to term. Buoyed, Mike and I went ahead with the operation.

Although the surgery went well and I was able to get pregnant six months later, the pregnancy was difficult. I bled periodically and had to spend the next five months in bed. When things gradually improved, I was able to resume light duties.

We thought things would be fine after that. One night after Mike was finishing his final exams at a local university, though, Mike heard a voice telling him to return to our apartment at once. When he came home, I was bleeding heavily. They rushed me to the hospital, where I lost almost six pints of blood.

I knew the baby had died but that I was still alive. I looked up from the hospital delivery room to see a man in a white robe standing at my feet. He assured me that everything from that point on would be fine; "I have conquered death," He said as he vanished.

I spent several months in therapy trying to find some ground on which to build hope. The prospects of this loss happening again were fairly high. But I had to create a future from what I didn't expect.

In the next two years, I began teaching adults English as a Second Language at a local Air Force base. I received several awards and felt motivated to work towards another degree. Mike and I realized that adoption was the best route to parenthood. We adopted a three-year-old boy who had been in several foster homes and was the victim of neglect and abuse. As teachers, we believed that early education, constructive discipline, and nurturing would enable John to overcome these early handicaps. When John was five, however, we learned that earlier trauma had rendered him emotionally disturbed. He had a personality disorder that could be modified through psychological therapy, special education, and tough love. But he could not live a fully productive life.

Not long before John's diagnosis, I got pregnant again. Realizing that both me and the baby might die, Mike and I decided to terminate the pregnancy. What gave us hope was that things would turn around for John. We had to wait almost seven years of treatment before we saw significant behavioral changes in John. When we saw this, Mike and I decided to adopt another child. This time, however, because we were over 35, national agencies turned us down. We eventually adopted a fourteen-month Guatemalan orphan, whom we named Nathaniel Michael.

Nate was intellectually gifted, and took active roles in scouting, baseball, and soccer. He delighted us continually. But Nate learned when he was in college that he had autism. Although it has restricted his social and vocational pursuits, Nate developed a business role. He became the business manager for a creative arts business, Art for the Spirit, which I opened two years ago following retirement from federal government; he directs all pricing, advertising and marketing.

Losing children and adopting two changed my views of parenthood, of myself, and of God. It began with the death of what I had believed about parenthood. Having children, whether biological or through adoption, did not validate or negate your value as a human being. Parents, moreover, despite their best intentions, could not set their children on the "best" or "right" paths; only children could do this. This freed me from the belief that I could control my children's choices. You may give them reasons and incentives otherwise, but they decide the paths they want to travel. They make mistakes and don't turn their lives around as you would like or expect. You need not feel demeaned or guilty; you can see beyond these things and be ready to welcome them back when things eventually turn around.

I began to see parenthood as God the Father might view it: through our free choices and wrong decisions, we try to control our own futures. To some extent, we do. But God still loves us and works to bring us out of what we may have gotten ourselves into. And although we were created through our biological parents, our relationship to God the Father comes through His adopting us through grace and its lifelong work. Parents are guardians of that grace.

The transformation, however, didn't diminish my anguish at losing children. I somehow knew they were with God and were alive. But I continued to wonder what they would have been like had they lived.

I got a glimpse the year after my husband died unexpectedly. Mike had had a heart condition, compounded by stage four pancreatic cancer following exposure to Agent Orange in Vietnam. One of the hardest things I had to do was cut off the oxygen during his final labored breaths in the hospital. It was like the therapeutic abortion over 40 years earlier all over again.

But I knew there was no hope. God had other plans for the one I loved and had to say goodbye to.

I thought the story had ended there. But one evening before going to sleep, I rolled over in my bed and happened to see a picture emerge on the floor. In a split second, I could see Mike as a young man chasing a blond-haired little boy that looked a lot like him. Now I know.

Carol Rusaw is a certified coach, organizational development consultant, trainer, and artist and enjoys helping people develop new perspectives on themselves, their relationships, their careers, and issues they are facing. With over 20 years' professional experience in these areas, she has a Doctor of Education, Masters of Theological Studies, Masters of Public Administration, Master of Arts in Education, and a Bachelor of Arts in English.

"Incredible Love Awesome Grace"

by Chinwe Chimezie Uwaoma

Incredible Love

Incredible love
Irresistible love
Amazing love
Love that translates from the dominion of darkness to light
What a love!
Love that has made us partakers of the divine nature
What a love!
Love that heals the broken hearted
Incredible love!

Love so wide
Love so long
Love so high
Love so deep
Love that forgives the vilest sinner
What a love!
Love that gives eternal life
Incredible love!
Love that accepts you into the beloved
Awesome love!

Love so lavished on us
As you behold this love
You are changed into the same image
From glory to glory
What a love!
Awesome love
Irresistible love
Incredible love!!

Awesome Grace

Grace, Grace, Grace
Glorious Grace
Given to us in the one He loves
Lavished with all wisdom and understanding
Awesome Grace!

Oh Grace!
Full of incomparable riches
Freely given to us by God
Expressed in his kindness to us by Christ Jesus
Awesome Grace!

Oh throne of Grace!
Beckons you to come boldly
As you prostrate wholeheartedly
To its Lordship
You will receive mercy forgiveness
Salvation and justification
Awesome Grace!
(Culled from "God In Plain Sight")

Chinwe Chimezie Uwaoma the wife of Pastor Chimezie .C. Uwaoma is an author/writer and a songwriter with a strong Christian heritage. She lives in Port Harcourt Nigeria with her husband and two children.

"Grief Chasing Gratitude"

by Rick Prashaw

Excerpt from Father Rick, Roamin' Catholic, Friesen Press, February 2022. (Adam is Rick's son who drowned at 22 after a seizure)

"…Adam and I had frequently texted when he lived in Ottawa. Now, occasionally, from wherever, I get a clear text from him that moves down the top centre part of my head. He is in good humour, in a good place, I sense. Better than where I find myself some days.

I want more. I want Adam in the flesh. My grief chases gratitude though to new, unthinkable chapters as a transgender human rights and organ donor advocate, an author, and storyteller breathing life into Adam and my corpses.

It's not all up, up, and away. I clutch the urn on dark nights of the soul. That's the reality check on the permanent mourning facing the bereaved. Forget what people say, best intentions and all. There is no getting over it. Mourning has no clock nor calendar. We are lifers.

Did you know there is no word in the English language to define a parent who loses a child?

We know whom orphans miss and whom a widow mourns.
There are no words to describe a parent who mourns a child.
In parish work, I had facilitated a Death and Dying ministry. Training began by listening to tapes outlining Elizabeth Kubler Ross's five stages of grieving, followed by participants sharing their own experiences with loss, all to shape future ministry. Kubler-Ross identified five stages then: denial, anger, bargaining, depression, and acceptance. She has since identified more stages or emotions. She never intended them as any logical, consecutive stages forward.
Life, people, and especially our feelings are never so neat. Broken hearts, the valleys, loneliness, jumbled and jarring reminders that Adam is dead, gone, all debilitating alongside dawns breaking, whiffs of renewal and hope.

Grief chasing gratitude. This is all sacred ground. I feel no urge to fix it.

As a priest, I had spoken to people in mourning about time helping to turn down the volume of the grieving, moving the hurt to corners in the room.

There is truth in that. Nonetheless, the mourning is forever because the love is forever. It feels like a muddy goo to wallow in and get stuck in too. It can be exhausting. I managed somehow to write Adam's and my first memoir in the depths of grieving. It was a lifeline that almost killed me.
As I signed books, there were moments I swear I was back in ministry.

"My son died about twenty years ago, your son's age, after a gunshot wound," a woman whispered. "He had the most beautiful blue eyes."

I blinked, imagining those beautiful eyes.

"My son was stillborn," another woman confessed, leaning over the signing table. "People don't understand my sadness."
Five years and counting. There is his presence and his absence. I remember Adam intentionally, less he is forgotten. I concoct complicated bank and business passwords that reflect Adam's story. I avoid anything experts label as harmful denial. I gave Adam's Carey Price Habs jersey to John Dickhout, Adam's heart recipient.

There is welcomed respite from the grieving, new life and energy, surprises beyond the stopgap, useful remedies of keeping busy and moving forward. It works for a while.

Freedom is what we do with what is done to us.

Jean-Paul Sartre's words work my bones. Past the fury and unanswered questions, an invitation beckoned. My father had lived Sartre's wisdom. Dad found his freedom past his being scared as an orphan and a soldier. His blood flowed through me to Adam, who likewise could wink back at woe. I admired both Dad and Adam for choosing life, for not being afraid. I try this. I hope others can as well. This is not a "take two aspirins, choose life" prescription.

Life can be menacingly tough.

Bittersweet, not bitter nor cynical. I ran from despair. Doors to gratitude opened.

Rick Prashaw is a Canadian author (Ottawa) with a diverse career as a journalist, Catholic priest, executive director of a national criminal justice NGO, and political staff to members of Parliament.

"A Blessing for this Time"

by Karen Wicker

May you know this…

Your quiet sobs are echoing with the sobs of all who despair
in a resounding cry for justice.

Your many tears are joining with the tears of all who weep
into an overflowing river of compassion.

Your deep heartache is connecting with the heartache of all who
mourn in a tender bond of companionship.

Your individual futility is uniting with the futility of all who lament to
become a force for good.

Your anguished longing is expanding with the longing of all who
yearn to serve as a vessel of greater peace.

Your unanswered questions are universal questions
and the answer is always love.

Your trembling feet are still standing in the presence of God
and you are on holy ground.

*Karen Wicker is a spiritual writer who shares meditations on her blog
site, <u>https://simplysoulsearching.com</u>. Since her time with cancer, she appreciates
these bonus days to spend with family and friends, walk in nature, and write her
contemplative memoir.*

"In Joy, Yet Grief"

by Devin Parrish

I thought I was doing fine until the night before graduation. A small group of close friends and family from all over the country joined me at a beautiful Airbnb in Minnesota for the ceremony. Some of us hadn't seen each other in years, others were meeting for the first time. It had been so much fun driving back and forth to the airport, picking people up, coming back to the house, staying up late engaging in spirited conversations, eating, and laughing. We even took a few group trips to some Twin Cities landmarks and Paisley Park despite the mostly cloudy, rainy, and cold weather.

On the eve of getting my Master's in Biblical Studies, my cousin Malikah came to check on me as I was configuring what to wear to walk across the stage and receive my degree. The door to my room was open and Malikah stuck her head in and called my name. When I turned around she asked, "Are you ok?" The tears poured forth, relieved that a secret longing in my soul to be asked that exact question had been fulfilled. I must've looked like I was going to collapse as I answered, "no" because Malikah quickly walked to the edge of my bed and we both fell down on it. I do not remember when or how she closed the bedroom door. I only remember crying on her shoulder, hard.

"I wish my mom was here for this," I finally said out loud as each word punched my sternum on the way out. A new round of grief from missing my mom all over again began then and persists as I write this essay.

I grieve daily and I have for most of my life. When I was a child, my family and I moved from city to city and state to state. I was always saying goodbye to friends, to routines, to comfort and bracing for the initial high of anticipating letters in the mail and the eventual low of those letters trailing off. As an adult, I started grieving differently. Friendships ended more because of emotional growth in different directions and less because of physical distance.

There's something else about the way I grieve now, especially how I grieve my mother.

In the initial years after her death, I missed her in an all-consuming way. It had more to do with her inaccessibility, that I couldn't call or visit her anymore. I grieved for loved ones before Mom. My maternal grandfather was the first significant death I experienced when I was 12. My paternal grandmother died a month before Mom and there were teachers, mentors, and other loved ones who preceded her.

But when you experience astronomical love with someone, when they leave this earth, you can find yourself wishing they were around for the good stuff like buying your first home, taking a life-changing trip, watching your first play being performed on stage, getting your master's degree in Biblical Studies. The absence of Mom's voice from the chorus of cheers after these accomplishments is just as overwhelming now as it was more than a decade ago.

Another kind of grief I recently experienced did not involve death, but its inevitability. I spent about two weeks with my favorite aunt and uncle (Mom's youngest brother), both of whom are in their late 70s. I hadn't seen them in person since they celebrated their 50th anniversary in 2018 and we made up for lost time.

Ahead of my visit, I told Uncle Bill, "All I want to do is rest. Don't plan anything, we don't have to run all over the place. I just want to spend time with you and Aunt Supat and rest." They honored my request. Besides interacting with a few folks who stopped by to visit or drop off a dish, there were days I didn't even leave the house, save for time spent playing with their beautiful dog in their huge yard.

We laughed, shared stories and memories and watched Aunt Supat's Thai shows on Netflix and there were other mundane activities like going to the grocery store. The morning I was preparing to come back home, I felt my eyes well up with tears. I fought it initially but when we stood in a circle to pray, I lost it. Aunt Supat kept saying, "You have to visit more often. We're getting older."

Uncle Bill and Aunt Supat's mortality wasn't at the forefront of my mind like my mother's.

Mom had many health challenges related to her heart throughout my life before she succumbed to pancreatic cancer. Although I've watched Uncle Bill and Aunt Supat age, they've always worked out. They still do, but over the last few years they've both had diagnoses and surgeries that slowed them down a bit. While we were standing in that prayer circle, the thought of them not being on earth anymore engulfed me. The urgency of Aunt Supat's plea to come visit them more often engulfed me and I cried. Her back-to-back hugs before Uncle Bill drove me to the airport made me sob.

That moment may have been the first time I'd ever really imagined what life would be like without them. Is there such a thing as pre-grieving? That's what I've started doing. See, it's not just thinking about them dying, it's thinking about the end of their tangible essence. The *hang*, you know? Spending time with them in that unique way where even the air around you suspends differently. After they're gone, they take their part of the air with them.

I can do all the mind tricks in an attempt to soften the blow of when that day comes again, but it won't work. Joy and grief will keep intersecting until they morph into a new way to cope with a loved one not being around anymore. I don't know if my joy will ever be the same as I brace for this approaching reality in the meantime.

Devin Parrish's storytelling shows up throughout her life as a writer, journalist, essayist, playwright, and YouTuber. She hopes to complete her PhD in Womanist Theology in the near future.

"From the Beginning"

by K.A. Hall

Eden the womb,
floating full and warm,
effortlessly one.

The fall
that unannounced inexorable first
trauma down the birth
canal—this must
be the end—then
out—severed into
separateness.

The labor of drawing independent breath,
then howling: we did not ask for this.
Bereft, we begin.

God wonders at the miracle, born again,
and weeps at the loss, wishing they
could forever contain us safe—
but that is no life.

Knowing only now
that creating a universe was easy,
that making a creature in their image
is the hardest work, long after birth.

We will abandon them
without thought and,
eternally needy,
return without warning.

Repeat, repeat, repeat, repeat

God holds us to their breast
and does their best.

"K.A. Hall lives and writes on the sunny side of the San Francisco Bay Area. She believes that, in the words of Miguel de Unamuno, 'from your work you will be able one day to gather yourself.'"

"Consider It All Joy, One Day at a Time"

by Rachel Ophoff

In that moment, joy smelled like pine trees awakened by the sun. Tiger swallowtails, my favorite butterflies, flitted merrily, if somewhat erratically, amongst the flowers. God's own embrace, a warm summer breeze, wrapped around my shoulders. Well praise the Lord! June had arrived.

The trail from our campsite down to lake meandered through an aspen grove. Folding chairs hung over our shoulders. Kevin carried the fishing poles, and I toted the tackle box. His book and my e-reader rode along in our backpacks. All this stuff was a little heavy for a vintage couple like us, but we're used to it. Together we've weathered forty Colorado winters just to take full advantage of our high-country summers.

Everything was perfect. The jagged peaks of the South San Juans pierced the deep blue sky over the lake. We found a great spot in the shade. Time to kick back, cast out our lines, and bury our noses in a good summer read.

I hit the button and waited. I shook my tablet from side to side. Then up and down. A brief message flickered before the screen went totally blank.

"Kevin, my pad is down to 6% power. This can't be happening. I charged it all night."

"Did you put it on airplane mode when we left town?"

Nuts. We left the pavement twenty-seven miles and several hours ago, blowing out of Dodge and into the wilderness. No people, no buildings, no cell service, no internet, no electricity. My device must have spent the day wandering the airwaves, searching for service. Poor little thing just wore itself out.

It's not like I have to be constantly entertained, but let's face it, three days of looking at scenery is a long time. To be fair, the view was breathtaking. Birdsong trilled through the pines. Ospreys circled overhead. Sunlight shone through the feathers of a soaring red-tailed hawk. Chipmunks scurried through the rocks. Mirror images of the Rocky Mountains reflected across the lake's glassy surface. People spend thousands to vacation where I live year-round. Who could get bored with this?

Sadly, me. About twenty minutes later.

Kevin had the good sense to bring a paper book, so he relaxed in the shade and waited for the fish to bite.

And I went to retrieve the only paper book I keep in the camper.

***

One year it dawned on me that I never took my Bible camping. Rather than adding it to my packing list, I decided to stash my Recovery Bible in the camper permanently. With all the versions we keep in the house, I thought it would be special to use something different in the wild. You know, fresh air, fresh perspective.

Still, three days. Not only is that a long time to look at the scenery, it's also a long time to spend reading the Bible. There's also the fact that, at the moment, my spiritual life is complicated. We're still solid on the basics: God is good, and He doesn't change. Jesus is the love of my life: the strength of my heart and my portion forever. The Holy Spirit comforts my soul and never leaves me for a moment. I'm loved, and I'm free.

But a terrible thing happened a while back, and it's still messing with my serenity.

The Evangelical Christian Church overwhelmingly supported the election of Donald Trump. I was devastated. The church was my family. I came to them broken and they showed me Jesus; in His care, and through their actions, I found healing. Words cannot express the depth of my grief. I should know. I've spent the last six years mopping tears off my keyboard. I thought if words could help, maybe they could fix it. Writing and praying were all I knew to do. My fury found an outlet, but my heart is still in pieces.

Jesus has healed me before, and the first time was a doozy. I just don't know if He can heal this.

***

I was born in the dark. Not the literal dark, but in a family shattered by violence. My father was a bipolar, alcoholic WWII vet with PTSD. My mother worked constantly to provide for us, but poverty and hopelessness held us hostage. That furnace was all I knew. Sheer survival was all I had. Then one night when I was fifteen, I got high for the first time.

Magic seemed to hang in the air as we crammed into the cavernous concert hall. The lights went down, the music came up, and the first chords of a screaming guitar shook the floor itself. As beams of light shot from the stage, thousands of teens screamed their approval. The party was on. The walls themselves thrummed to the beat. Acrid smoke wafted by.

Out of the shadows someone passed me a joint.

I didn't even think twice. I sucked in the scorching heat and held my breath as long as I could.

Then I exhaled my innocence.

Time seemed to soften as I felt my brain lifting from my body, wrapped in a warm, gray blanket. A lifetime's worth of emotional pain floated off into the smoky haze. I was home. The first words out of my mouth were, "where can I get more of this?"

So began a seventeen-year love/hate affair with drugs and alcohol. As we say in recovery, I was off to the races. For those of us who get drunk or high to ease the pain in our souls, the races take us places we'd never planned on going. Mine took me to Colorado.

✳✳✳

To most people, the term "geographic" refers to a study of the features of the Earth. Many folks in recovery crack a wry smile when we hear the word, because 'doing a geographic' means moving away to fix our problems. We figure that, because our troubles couldn't possibly be our fault, they must lie with the people/places/things that cause us to self-medicate. Therefore, the farther away, the better.

So I moved from Miami to Aspen. "What a great idea!" said no one, ever. Aspen's nightlife was party central. I didn't set out to become an addict or an alcoholic. No one does. It's just that I had found a pudding-headed peace, and there was no way I was going back.

The only problem? I couldn't stay high all the time. I had to make a living. In an astounding intervention by a God I was yet to meet, I found a job as a bookkeeper. A kind-hearted woman desperately wanted to go on vacation and needed someone to fill in, so I was hired. Since mental impairment wreaks havoc in bookkeeping, I needed to act like a normal person. At least during the day.

My boss and I would get to talking over work, just getting acquainted and all friendly-like. Then one day this zinger came out of nowhere.

"Do you know Jesus?"

Did I know Jesus? How could I tell her, with absolute certainty and no small amount of trepidation, that Jesus would not want to know me? I thought all she saw was a twenty-three-year-old woman with a head for numbers and a pulse. I figured if she really knew me, she wouldn't have bothered to ask. She would have known I wasn't the Jesus type.

✳✳✳

I also used to think miracles occurred instantaneously, destined only for the holy who deserved God's favor. Never in my wildest dreams could I envision a miracle that took seven years, much less one that happened to me. And yet, this quiet woman started praying for me. She didn't just see an employee; she saw me as a daughter of the King. She also befriended me. I was not a friend she needed. Our lifestyles were wildly dissimilar. She was a respected church lady, community leader, and entrepreneur; I was a party animal. She started praying for me to know Jesus.

For seven years I drove past the church before I got the courage to go in. Three years after that I got clean and sober. Reading the Word fed the cravings of my soul. Jesus became real. Old wounds slowly healed. New wounds didn't kill me. When my daughter died, on a church trip no less, God suddenly seemed silent, distant, and cruel. I refused to let go. Scouring the Bible for answers, I beat on His chest with one fist and clung to Him with the other. Together, we navigated the deep waters of grief, of belief, and eternal hope.

And all the while, what I believed was the body of Christ, the Evangelical Christian Church, stood with me in the gap between Heaven and Earth. Never could I have imagined I would walk away.

But in 2020, after four years of trying to reason with a congregation of Trump supporters in a rural town full of MAGA churches, Kevin and I said our goodbyes. I still trust God; I'm just not sure about some of His kids.

***

Back in the camper I dug out my Bible, as well as a tattered devotional magazine. Thumbing through it brought tears to my eyes. The woman I was when I read it last was open and eager, naively and joyously involved in Christian community. Plunking myself back down in my camp chair, I reeled in my line, checked my bait, and asked the Lord what He wanted me to see. Flipping through the pages, this title grabbed me by throat:

"When Our Faith Wavers"

When our faith wavers? This can't be the one. My faith hasn't wavered in years. Sure, though my faith in some of God's people is kaput, I still know a few things for sure: God doesn't change. Jesus Christ is the same yesterday, today, and forever. All my hope clings to that Rock. What was I missing?

Reading further, the familiar words of James 1: 2-4 (NIV) literally made me scowl.

> *Jas 1:2* *Consider it pure joy, my brothers, whenever you face trials of many kinds,*
> *Jas 1:3* *because you know that the testing of your faith develops perseverance.*
> *Jas 1:4* *Perseverance must finish its work so that you may be mature and complete, not lacking anything.*

Really? We're here again? Hebrews 11:1 (NIV) defines faith as, "being sure of what we hope for and certain of what we do not see." Jesus, you know I've got this. I could never have survived Catherine's death without it. My hope lives in heaven. What more do you want from me?

"Perseverance must finish its work so that you may be mature and complete, not lacking anything."

Ah, you mean the wound that won't seem to heal.

"Perseverance must finish its work…"

Lord, you know I've prayed about this forever. I don't know what else to do.

"…so that you may be mature and complete, not lacking anything."

Jesus, no disrespect intended, but good luck with that. I'm not even sure you can fix me.

***

As the sun headed for the horizon, we packed up our gear and hiked back up the hill. The trout had outsmarted us, successfully avoiding capture for the entire afternoon.

Kevin lit the charcoal, and I prepped dinner. I couldn't stop thinking about what I'd heard from God. He knows my heartache. He knows how hard I've prayed for a solution. But, then again, He knows me. He is familiar with all my ways, including my process for working through grief. I wish I could miraculously bridge the disconnect between His thinking and mine. For now, I only know this:

I miss the woman I used to be. I loved and trusted my church family. Together we laughed and cried and grieved and rejoiced and celebrated. We camped and cleaned and gave each other a lot of grace. With the hands we raised in worship we cooked each other meals, played with each other's kids, and dried each other's tears. Together we were the family I had always longed for.

I miss who I was.

I miss those people.

I wonder if I'll ever find that kind of family again.

I have no clue how to heal from this heartache. Even "finding it pure joy," will be quite a stretch.

***

After dinner, we sat around the fire and watched the stars come out. Far above sea level and even farther from city lights, the Milky Way spills out like a handful of diamonds God tossed our way. To call it breathtaking is an understatement. It is magnificent.

> *Ps 19:1 The heavens declare the glory of God;*
> *the skies proclaim the work of his hands.*

Despite my fear of bears in the bushes, I stay awake as long as I can. I'm transfixed by the darkening sky. Billions of stars burn in the Milky Way alone. Billions of galaxies burn across eternity. While my poor brain is whining about loneliness, God's got a lot on His plate.

And yet, He hears my every prayer. He sees my every tear. He knows that all will be well eventually. He wants me to trust Him with every step, beginning again with what I heard today.

For all I know, joy may come again tomorrow morning. Maybe this time it will smell like coffee.

Rachel Ophoff is incredibly grateful that Jesus Christ is the same yesterday and today and forever, and she's simply astonished that he loves her. She shares their stories at <u>https://rachelophoff.com</u>.

"And It is Said"

by Ronald Kevern

I awaken every morning, with my focus to the sky:
   there are Prayers inside my heart; they start always with a sigh.

Between my God and Heaven, without a plan I pray
   Always first in this man's mind, I thank God for this day.

Even before a day is started; somedays on my knees;
   I ask my God to help me find ways to please.

Lifting my eyes to the Heavens, & knowing God is there
   Sometimes I feel a tender touch & I know that God does care.

I think of all my family, my wife and mom and dad
   Who all reside in Heaven; that does not make me sad.

Every day I feel their presence; they have a home I know;
   Because my Bible tells me and this I know tis so.

Very much I love my children, and that God already knows;
   I pray for homeless and hungry and for all of those in woe.

Even as I close my morning prayer; and struggle at the end;

I know my prayers are heard, and I close with an Amen.

(If you take the first letter of each verse, you will know the prayer I
weave,   It's not only because I awaken; I it is said cause I BELIEVE!)

Ronald Kevern is a 90-year-old retired educator who lives in Arizona. His BA and MA were earned at Central Michigan University and the U of M. Ron has three children, eleven grandchildren and two great granddaughters. He is a member of the Pleasantville N.Y. Presbyterian Church and also an affiliate member At the Pinnacle Presbyterian Church in Scottsdale, AZ.

www.ingramcontent.com/pod-product-compliance
Lightning Source LLC
Chambersburg PA
CBHW071440300726
48976CB00004B/1404